Table of Contents

Disclaimer .... pg 4

Acknowledgement .... pg 6

What is a Reverse Mortgage .... pg 9

What Have You Heard About Reverse Mortgages .... pg 13

Forward Mortgage Comparisons .... pg 17

Myths of Reverse Mortgages .... pg 23

Retirement vs Inheritance vs Qualify of Life .... pg 27

Looking into Your Future, Your Financial Future, and Your Family's Future .... pg 31

Financial Alternatives for Seniors .... pg 35

What are the Options to Seniors in Life .... pg 39

Consequences of Waiting to get a Reverse Mortgage .... pg 45

Non Borrowing Spouse Rules .... pg 47

Elder Abuse & Elder Financial Abuse .... pg 51

Seniors vs Adult Children .... pg 59

Can a Reverse Mortgage be
Foreclosed .... pg 63

Grey Divorce & Seniors .... pg 67

Credit Line Growth Factor .... pg 71

How to Help Senior Parents .... pg 75

So, You Want to Leave the House
to Your Kids? .... pg 79

Pass Equity Before you Die .... pg 85

Sandwich Generation .... pg 89

Why do Reverse Mortgages Require
Counseling & Forward Mortgages
Don't? .... pg 93

The HECM for Purchase Program
for Retirees .... pg 97

What Happens After Death.
    What Heirs & Family Must Know ... pg 101

Estate Planning Issues for People
with Pets .... pg 111

Seniors with Pets, What to do? .... pg 116

Proposed Changes for 2020 .... pg 123

Second Appraisal Requirement .... pg 127

State of Nevada Living Will Lockbox ..... pg 131

Final Thoughts .... pg 135

About the Author .... pg 139

Disclaimer

This book is designed to provide information on reverse mortgages. It is published with the understanding that the publisher and author are not engaged in rendering legal, financial, or other professional services. If legal or other expert assistance is required, the services of a competent professional should be sought.

The purpose of this book is not to reprint all of the information that is otherwise available about reverse mortgages, but to complement, amplify and supplement other information on the subject. Every effort has been made to make the text herein as complete and accurate as possible. However, there may be mistakes or outdated information in the content. Therefore, this text should be used only as a general guide and not as the ultimate source of reverse mortgage information. The information contained in this book about reverse mortgages are current up to the publication date. The author assumes no responsibility for errors, inaccuracies, the omissions, the or inconsistencies.

The author of this book shall have neither liability nor responsibility to any person or entity with respect to any loss or damage caused, or alleged to have been caused, directly or indirectly, by the information contained in this book. The author is not endorsing any reverse mortgage product, options available, or any specific lender.

Acknowledgement

This is the third book I write on Reverse Mortgages and it has been a great pleasure to spend countless hours gathering ideas, facts, and putting it all together for your learning pleasure. I sincerely hope all readers will take the time to learn about this great Federal Program for Seniors and implement the Program into your life.

I want to give thanks to all my co-workers and friends who have supported me in writing this venture and put up with me throughout the months which it took me sitting at Dunkin Donuts with my computer formulating each and every chapter of this book.

In addition, a special thanks to my friend Michael D. for all the questions he imposed on me which made me think outside the box and had me come up with many answers which I have used here in this book.

My sincere thanks to all.
George Lagarde

What is a Reverse Mortgage?

First, let's talk about what it is not.

The Reverse Mortgage of old, the one you hear about from your gardener, or your mechanic, or your neighbor, even your best friend; is not what the Reverse Mortgage is today!

It used to be that Bank would not only charge interest on the loan amount, but also took a large percentage (often up to 50%) of the remaining equity in your home after the loan was paid off. That meant the heirs would receive a lot less than expected after the loan was paid off.

This was not fair, and so the Federal Government stepped in and changed the guidelines, so the banks could not take more than the accumulated interest on the loan, and all the appreciation of the property would belong to the heirs.

This is the new Reverse Mortgage Program called HECM for Home Equity Conversion Mortgage. Today, the Seniors are completely protected from such practices, and so are their heirs. When the last borrower moves out of the house, or passes away, the loan is called, and what is due the bank is just the original loan balance plus all interest accrued over the time the Seniors have had the use of the Reverse Mortgage. All remaining equity belongs to the senior's estate, and their heirs. The bank does not retain any equity in the home.

In fact, since the seniors own the home, they can sell it anytime they wish, and move to another home, which (if they financially qualify) can purchase another home using the Reverse for Purchase Program.

One of the greatest benefits of the Program for me is the security it offers married seniors because the loan is on both lives, and as long as one senior/owner occupies the property the loan is in full effect. This means that should something happen to one spouse, nothing happens to the loan, and therefore, nothing happens to the remaining spouse.

I see this as a great feature because in many cases where a senior pass or goes into an assisted living or nursing home, the other spouse loses one income, but must continue to pay on the current "forward" mortgage even though they have lost one income. And, in many cases, the remaining spouse cannot make the payment and eventually loses the home to foreclosure or is forced to sell it.

That cannot happen with a Reverse Mortgage since the loan is on both spouses' lives. The only responsibility one has is to continue to pay the Real Estate taxes, homeowner insurance, any HOA fees, and maintain the property. That's it. Stay home and live your life without the worry of having to make a monthly mortgage payment.

What have you heard about Reverse Mortgages?

I'm sure most of you have "War Stories" to share with me. Mostly bad ones! And, most of you have your own definite opinions about the Program.

Well, I'm here to share some information which may shock you or may enlighten you, depending on how strong your believes are and if you want to learn the truth about the Program.

In the past 12 years of doing just Reverse Mortgages I have heard so many "untruths" you wonder why I am still in the business. Also, I have heard so many Seniors tell me that Reverse Mortgages are a "horrible" loan program to take out. Yet, my mother had one on her home for 6 years until she passed, and I have one on my own home today, and I am extremely happy with it. I guess it may make sense for some and not for others, and this is what I want to explain in this chapter.

Reverse Mortgages are NOT for everyone! It is also NOT for the poor and destitute, or as some have put it, "a loan of last resort". Throughout the years since 1989, there have been many changes to the Program and each has made it safer for the Seniors. Today, Seniors are more protected than they ever have been before. So, as they say, "this is not your Grandmother's Reverse Mortgage", is very true.

Why Seniors take out a Reverse Mortgage? There are so many reasons that you could write a book about it: well, I did, my first book where 100 Reasons Why Seniors Took Out a Reverse Mortgage". But let's just take a look at a few categories.

First, Seniors want to get rid of their current mortgage payment.

Second, Seniors want to have extra cash each month to live on.

Third, Seniors need to renovate, or upgrade their homes, make them more Senior friendly.

Fourth, Seniors want to help out their adult children with their debt burden. Ok, some do.

Fifth, Seniors want to Travel, or spend money on themselves, rather than to a bank.

Sixth, Seniors want to invest the extra cash they are entitled to, to make more money to live on.

Now, where do you fall in?

What I do not understand is why so many of us take advise from people who are not informed and who do not have an understanding of the changes that have been made over time, yet they easily volunteer their opinion onto others who are vulnerable to accept what is said, and not what could be learned?

This statement goes for those individuals who are considered professionals too. For instance, there are many Attorneys, Financial Planners, and CPA's who have not taken the time to learn about the new changes and yet spew out erroneous information from what they believe to still be a fact without even giving any thought to educate themselves of the new changes affecting the Program and the Seniors they counsel. It also stands for those Seniors who take advice from non-professionals such as a neighbor, a friend, or a relative. Or, how many times have I heard, "my gardener told me", or, my "mechanic mentioned", or even "the cable guy said", yet we all wish to accept these

Forward Mortgage Comparison with a Reverse Mortgage.

I would like to make a comparison of a product you most probably have, and trust, to a product which you may despise and most probably never recommend to anyone. Please bear with me.

If you own a home, and you have a mortgage on it, please read on. We have all grown up believing, trusting and knowing that when we want to buy a home, we go to a Bank, and apply for a mortgage. We do not give it a second thought. And the only thing we ask about is the "rate".

But, what do we really know about these mortgages? Other than we have to "get one" or else we do not own a house. I ask, who really owns the house? You or the Bank? Well, you do. The deed is in your name, not the Bank's. Yet the mortgage you signed gives a tremendous number of rights to the "Bank". Have you really sat down and read the mortgage document? Don't! You may not sleep at nights for the next 30 years.

Here are some points which I would like to enlighten you with.

First: Yes, you own the house, but the Bank owns you.

Second: You must make a monthly payment.

Third: If you miss three payments, they will start a foreclosure on "your" house.

Fourth: You have the right to sell the house at any time you want, but first you must pay back the Bank the amount owed to them. Any remainder is "yours". This fact is obvious, and most of us know this.

Fifth: When you got the mortgage, you qualified with both your incomes. What happens if one of you gets sick, goes in a nursing facility, or passes on? The Bank does not care; the payment is due the first of each month, no matter what. However, if you lose one income, will the remaining spouse have enough income to continue to pay the mortgage each month, and still have enough to live on? My experience is that it becomes extremely difficult for that remaining spouse to continue to live in the manner they are accustomed to. And, most likely will be forced to use up all kinds of savings, investments, or even sell the house to get rid of that mortgage payment with only one income.

So, I ask, today, would you be able to qualify for the mortgage amount you have with only one income? Most likely not, so why not learn about other means of financing available to you and your family to protect you, your loved one, and your family from being forced to do the unthinkable and be forced to get rid of your home?

Sixth: What will you want to happen when you and your spouse pass? Probably, you would want the house to go to your kids. But, let's be honest, do your kids actually want to live in your house? Most likely they have their own homes and have their own families. So, they will likely sell your house and pay off your current mortgage and keep the rest of the money for themselves. Remember, your kids will not want your home, they want the money from your home!

Many of us Seniors, want to leave so much "house" to our kids, that we prevent ourselves from having a great and rewarding retirement so we can leave as much "equity" to our kids as possible. I trust most of us would age better if we did not have to worry about finances and have enough money to do whatever we would like to do in retirement.

Okay, so allow me to introduce a product I love, I have for myself, even had one for my mother, and possibly recommend for your you. I know off the bat, you will hate me for this, but please, I urge you to listen, and learn, and investigate it before you close your mind to it and reject it wholeheartedly.

That is, the Reverse Mortgage product. Not the one you may have heard about 10, 15 or 20 years ago, but the new Program Insured by the Federal Government which today is helping out so many Seniors stay in their homes and continue to have a string financial future.

Let's take a look at some points:

First: You own your home.

Second: You do NOT have to make any monthly payments. And, by all means, don't fall behind.

Third: Your responsibility is to pay your taxes, homeowners' insurance, any HOA, and maintain the property. But, this is the same as with a regular mortgage, no?

Fourth: You have the right to sell your home any time you want. The mortgage balance is paid off, and the rest is yours. Same as with a regular mortgage too.

Fifth: With a reverse mortgage you have all the same rights as with a regular mortgage, but without the obligation of making a payment. In fact, you may have more rights than with a regular mortgage. A reverse can be refinanced in the future (you must qualify). You may be able to sell your home, and purchase another home using a reverse mortgage (again, you must qualify). And, what I consider the most important fact; that if one spouse gets sick, goes into a nursing facility or passes, the remaining spouse does not have to do a thing! That spouse has the right to remain in the property for as long as they want, again without having to make any payments. Does your current mortgage offer your family this protection?

So, I ask you not to have a negative judgment about the reverse mortgage product, and let's get together and learn about how it really works, and how it may help you in the future vs how your current mortgage "will" affect your family in the future.

George Lagarde
702-845-4632
ReverseGeorge@gmail.com

Myths of Reverse Mortgages

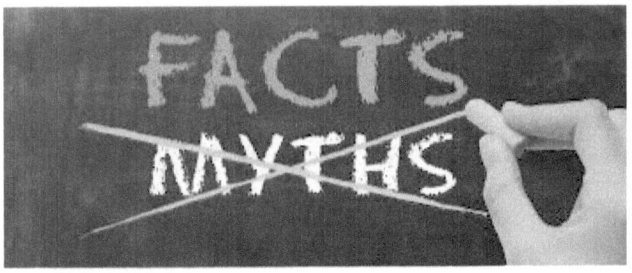

1. I WOULD BE SELLING MY HOUSE TO THE BANK

FALSE: You keep the title to your house. The lender will add a lien on the property, but you will still have complete control over it.

2. MY HEIRS WON'T INHERIT ANYTHING

FALSE: Your estate only owes the balance on the reverse mortgage. The balance is however much you've spent and interest. Let's say you got a reverse mortgage and owed $50,000 after 5 years. Then you decided to sell the house for $250,000. The lender gets $50,000 and you get $200,000.

3. I MIGHT "OUTLIVE" THE LOAN

FALSE: FHA/HUD reverse mortgages are designed specifically so that you can't outlive the loan. When you get the reverse mortgage, the lender will charge you a nominal fee to purchase FHA mortgage insurance. That insurance guarantees that even if you live to be 100, you can never owe more than the value of your home and you can never be forced to leave.

4. I COULD GET FORCED OUT OF MY HOME

FALSE: FHA/HUD reverse mortgages specifically state that you cannot be forced out of your home.

5. SOCIAL SECURITY AND MEDICARE WILL BE AFFECTED

FALSE: Money from a reverse mortgage is not considered income because it is a loan. For this reason, a reverse mortgage does not lower Social Security and Medicare benefits. It may on SSI and Medicaid benefits.

6. I WOULD HAVE TO PAY TAXES ON THE REVERSE MORTGAGE

FALSE: You already paid taxes on the money when you were putting the equity into your home. When you take it out again, it is not taxable.

7. THERE ARE BIG OUT-OF POCKET EXPENSES

FALSE: Most of the costs are financed into the loan. The only out-of-pocket expenses is for the Counseling fee (if charged) and the appraisal.

8. A REVERSE MORTGAGE IS SIMILAR TO A HOME EQUITY LOAN.

FALSE:

(a) Home equity loans may have many requirements such as high income, low debt, and good credit that a reverse mortgage does not. (b) You can "outlive" a home equity loan and end up being foreclosed on by the bank. This can never happen with a reverse mortgage. (c) A reverse mortgage usually has significantly lower interest rates.

Retirement vs Inheritance vs Qualify of Life.

Planning for Retirement vs Planning for Quality of Life, vs Planning to leave an Inheritance?

Where do you stand? If you are in, or nearing Retirement, you will pick (even if by default) one of these choices for the way you will live in your Senior years.

So, let's take a look at each. You have worked all your life, saved up, maybe even invested some of your money wisely, and you think this is the money you will use as your retirement income. What is that amount? Figure it out yourself. But, make sure it's a realistic figure, and in a monthly amount.

Secondly, will you be forced to make a Life Status change? Or a Quality of Life change? That is, will you have to downsize your living standards? Will you have to sell your home and move in with your children, or perhaps into an apartment or condo? Will you have to be careful on what you spend your money, what you can and cannot buy? So, just how much will Retirement change your quality of life?

Third, how important is it for you to leave your home to your kids? Will it be the home for them to live in, or for them to sell, and keep the money? I have found that most Seniors who want to leave their "home" to their kids (including my mother) actually wanted to leave the house for them. But the children will want the money, not the house!

I remember having this discussion with my mother who lived in Florida, and she wanted to leave her "home" to me. Well, I lived in New York, where I had a job, my own family, and had my own home. So, did I need her house? No! And surely, I was not going to move to Florida to live in "her" house! It took a lot of conversations to convince her that I did not want her "home", but she was insistent that she had to leave me the house debt free when she died. And, at what cost to her, and her quality of life?

Maybe many of you feel the same was as my mother did, but the reality is this: During her lifetime, she could not afford to live by herself in her own home with her retirement income. So, as a good child, I was subsidizing her expenses each month. That was money coming out of my pocket and taking from my own family each month. Why? Just so I could get that money returned to me when she passed after I sold her home? This seemed like a ridiculous thing to do, so I looked into having her take out a reverse mortgage on her home, which gave her a monthly amount, and yes, I got less later when she passed, but it did not affect me or my family's personal finances each month while she  was alive. It was a win win situation for both of us. And, this day, I also have a reverse mortgage on my house in order to maintain my quality of life, and my daughters will get the remaining equity from my home when I pass. BTW: I cannot count on my two daughters to pay for my living expenses when I get older, they have their own financial issues.

Another twist I used when I took out my Reverse Mortgage, was to look into getting a $100,000 or $200,000 10 year Term Life Insurance Policy, and pay it from the proceeds of the Reverse Mortgage. Yes, my house is paying for my life insurance!

And, when I die, my daughters will not only inherit the equity left in my house but also the amount of the life insurance. So, I urge you to, again, to get informed and see what works best for you and your family.

So, I urge you to look into your retirement goals and projections and determine the best way you wish to live out your life in Retirement. If I can help you with your own situation to improve your quality of life to be more worthwhile, please give me a call, and I'm sure I can help sort things out!

George Lagarde
702-845-4632
ReverseGeorge@gmail.com

Looking into your future, your financial future and your family's future.

I wrote a book about the reasons why people have taken out a Reverse Mortgage, and I included 100 perspectives as to why people chose to pay off their mortgage and take out some of the equity in their homes to live with instead of depending on Social Security and their savings alone. One of the things I learned while reviewing these reasons is that people were not thinking ahead, today is today, and we know what is happening in our lives. But tomorrow is an unknown. Tomorrow we may be healthy, or get an illness, we may need assistance in the day to day activities of life, or we may even pass away.

Tomorrow is the biggest unknown in our lives, yet very few of us consider that anything may happen to us. This is like living with your head buried in the sand, because the one thing I found out while writing my book, is that life changes, and as we grow older our health will deteriorate. No matter how much exercise we do, or what healthy foods we eat, as the body ages things change in our lives. All we have to do is look at a picture of yourself when you were 20, when you were 30, when you were 40, and when you were 60, have you changed?

We must do the same thing when looking at the future and the remaining days we have on this earth because the one thing that is guaranteed, is that life as we know it will change as we get older. Another guarantee is: if you are married, one spouse will pass before the other. So, what are you leaving him/her with when you pass? Will it be a tremendous amount of money, a huge mortgage payment each month, a lifetime of worry-free goals for him/her to achieve, or a lifetime of worry, limited income, and instability in life?

I urge every single one of you to look into your future and determine, what we in the Army called: Plan A; stay healthy, Plan B; One gets an illness, and even Plan C; One passes away. And although you may not have a need to do things right away, outline for yourself what you would have to do to accomplish all three  plans in the event you need to implement it in the future.

One area that I want to emphasize is that of husband and wives and what happens to the healthy, remaining spouse, instead of the one who gets an illness or dies. More often than not, we worry about the husband getting sick, having to go into a hospital, or even an assisted facility, or even if they prematurely pass away. However, what happens to the remaining spouse? Have we ever given that much thought? For example, husband and wife live in a modest home with a mortgage on their home, and let's say they are paying $800 per month, and they have 12 years to pay on this mortgage. If the husband passes, what happens to that remaining spouse? Well, this is the point I would like to address here. Chances are the wife will lose her husband's Social Security income, perhaps she will lose any pensions he was receiving. 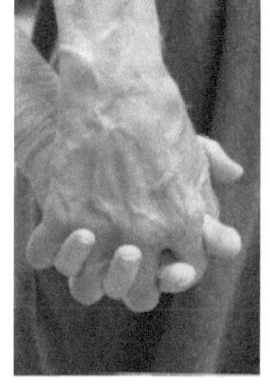 And she will find herself in a position where she is now living on half, or perhaps less, than the total income she had before her husband passed. However, the bills remain, the monthly housing expenses remain, and that pesky mortgage of $800 per month comes due the first of every month for the next 12 years. Will she have enough money to pay that each month? Will she have to use his life insurance money to pay off the mortgage? Will she have to dip into her investments to pay that mortgage payment? Will she have enough money to live on for the rest of her life? Or will she be forced to sell and move?

This is where thinking ahead for the future comes into play. Many Attorneys and Financial Planners today are seeing a value of the new Reverse Mortgages as a Financial Tool to alleviate a family before these issues arise, before one spouse passes, and before you have to spend your hard-earned retirement savings and have little left for your personal future.

The Reverse Mortgage gives a family the security of knowing that if anything happens to either spouse, the remaining spouse is set for life. That is to say, there is nothing that will affect the remaining spouse as far as their housing, because when one spouse passes, nothing happens to the reverse mortgage. It stays in effect just as before.

In addition, the remaining spouse knows she/he still owns the property, it can be refinanced, it can be sold, and if the remaining spouse wishes, and qualifies, she/he can purchase another home with a reverse mortgage.

Financial Alternatives for Seniors.

Many Senior Retirees in our Community have been tapping their savings and investments over the years in order to maintain a lifestyle they are accustomed to. In many cases, they are forced to go to a bank and apply for a mortgage, or second mortgage, or even an Equity Line of Credit in order to have extra cash available to live on each month. But with this move there are consequences. Let's look at just one example.

The first line of offense is the Bank when we need money. Yet, a Bank's philosophy is, "when you need money, we are not willing to give it to you". So, what do we do? When you approach a Bank for a loan, they will want to know your credit history, your income, your expenses, and mostly how you are going to repay them bank. So, they take a look at both your income and your spouse's income to evaluate if you can repay them. But here is where it gets tricky. If they give you a 30 year loan or a 20 year Heloc; how old are you today? If you are 65, 70, or even 80, chances are that you will be making a payment for the rest of your life. But what happens if 10 or 15 years down the road, when one of you gets sick, goes into a nursing home, or passes away? Yes, the remaining spouse MUST continue to make the same monthly payment for the next 10 or 15 years ahead. Frightening! But what we don't acknowledge is that when we lose a spouse, we also lose their income. The remaining spouse, with one income alone cannot afford to make the payments anymore and maintain some semblance of a lifestyle. So, the next month after your loss, the Bank comes knocking at your door like always demanding the monthly payment whether you can make it or not. In many cases, I have seen grieving spouses have to sell their homes because they can no longer make these payments with their sole income alone.

So, what can Seniors do? First, if you are in need of cash to live on, and your desire is to take out a second mortgage or refinance your first, or any kind of financing, I suggest trying to make the Bank qualify you using only one income. Why? Because if and when, and it will happen, one spouse passes, then by borrowing only that amount which one spouse can afford to pay each month, then he/she will still be able to stay in the home and make those payments without any difficulty. Will the Banks on their own do this? No way! They will never do it this way, unless you demand it. The Banks exist for the "here and now". They do not care about the future or you!

This is such a sad case that we must educate ourselves about it and become pro-active about getting these long-term loans when we are already in our Senior years of life. We must all do our due diligence and consult a Financial Planner, CPA, Elder Care Attorney, or a Mortgage Professional to find ways to resolve our financial situations without putting ourselves in such a dilemma that will hurt our spouse and the only way out is to sell the house and move...

What are the Options to Seniors in Life?

So often I meet with Seniors who ask me what their options in Retirement are to save money and have more money at the end of every month to live on.

Well, I have put together this article to show you what those options are and ideas to help you decide what to do with your lives. We must make a few assumptions:

First, you are currently paying off a mortgage on your home, or your home is free and clear.

Second; you are married, or you are single.

Third; you run out of money before the end of each month to live on, or you are independently wealthy and do not need any more money to live on.

Fourth; you want to live in your current home the rest of your life, or you are looking to move in the next 1-5 years.

These are some of the things I have heard over the last 10 years from Seniors:

1. I am healthy, I will not get sick.
2. We have "children" who will take us in and take care of us physically and financially.

3. My spouse will never die!
4. We will always have two incomes to cover our lifestyle!
5. Neither of us will never have a need to live in an Assisted Facility or Nursing Home!
6. I have plenty of money to live the rest of my life. How long is that?
7. We have to leave our house to our children. Is it the house, or the money from the house?

Your Options:

1. Do Nothing! Continue the lifestyle you have today. You have enough cash to pay all your monthly bills, and emergencies that life gives us. God bless you; I hope the best for you.
2. Use investments to live off and hope it never runs out.

3. Use your Savings & Investments to pay off any mortgage, or credit you owe now.
4. Continue to work, even part time, to make extra cash to cover bills.

5. Talk to your "children" and know how they feel about you getting old. Who will take care of you? Where will you live? Will you be on your own?
6. Buy a lot of Life Insurance to cover what you want to leave behind.
7. Find alternative sources of income to use in the style you are accustomed to.
8. Or, change your lifestyle so you can afford to live with the income you have.

Most people, either do nothing, and hope for the best, or they plan ahead and look to all the resources available to make a plan to cover many different contingencies of life. Where do you fall in? Are you the type to bury your head in the sand, or plan ahead?

Many of us who wish to plan ahead, are faced with a myriad of unknowns. Many of us do nothing, because it is too complicated to learn what the alternatives are, and what the ramifications might be. Or, even are discouraged because they think they may be making a mistake. Life is about learning and taking risks! You married your spouse, wasn't that a risk? Did it work? If it didn't, you looked for an alternative—a divorce, then you moved on. You bought a house; was it the best house on the market? Did you pay the cheapest price for it? Does it matter now, you live in it, it became your home. Well, life is just the same. We make decisions based on what we know and hope for the best. **TOUGH DECISIONS AHEAD** In retirement, we all must make decision way ahead of the time we will need to use them. I'm here to say that the one asset that we have that is the least understood is our homes! There are so many things you can do with your house, that it becomes scary to even think of the consequences, but I'm here to tell you that the one thing I do know, and do it very well, is to counsel you on those alternatives and how to use them.

One works hard all their lives to have a lifestyle, they marry, raise a family, save, invest, take many precautions, make some mistakes along the way, but we persevere. We have also worked hard to buy, maintain, & leave a home we have struggled at times to keep and pay off that mortgage. Now, in retirement, it's about time that house will pay you back and give you some peace of financial mind. Learn about the Reverse Mortgage Program, it really can work out for you!

Keep in mind that any financial decisions you make should be made with the help of a licensed financial advisor who can direct you best as to what to do with your retirement planning.

Retirement decisions is nothing more than: Knowledge over fear!

Someone said: If you don't plan, you are planning to fail. Well, I say: If you don't learn, you cannot plan, and if you don't plan, you are open to what the future will bring you.

Consequences of Waiting to get a Reverse Mortgage

Quite often I have heard Seniors tell me that they want to wait another year or two before they take out the Reverse Mortgage.

Why would they want to wait? Most likely, because they are confused about the Program, and as I have always said: "A Confused Mind Always Says No!" Or, perhaps I have not done my job properly and explained how the Program works. Or perhaps, they feel that by waiting, they will get a better deal a year or two from now.

In actuality, waiting will likely not give you a better Reverse Mortgage. You see, if you currently have a mortgage on your home, you will have another 12 or 24 months of having to make more payments. How much will that cost you? And, waiting may help you in that the value of your home may go up, but it may also go down? Are you so sure that will not happen? The Market is fickle! And, also, if there is a change by the FHA to the Reverse Mortgage Program at the Federal level, (as it has in the past few years) they may lower the PLF, which is the Factor by which they determine the amount of loan the

Government will give you, in a sense lowering your loan amount. Lastly, if the Government changes the qualification regulations (as they did two years ago) you may not qualify next year or the year after. So, as you can see, waiting may not be the smartest thing to do.

You may wait, pay more on your current mortgage, and get less from the Government next year although your home value may have gone up. Yes, that may just happen. In case you may be considering waiting, I suggest you get the facts today, and get the loan today, do not wait. What do they say: A bird in the hand…it applies here, and it is very true.

Non Borrowing Spouse Rules

What is meant by the term: Non-Borrowing Spouse?

This is a very misunderstood term when used within a Reverse Mortgage Loan. Most likely this comes about when a couple wanting to get a Reverse Mortgage and one spouse is over 62, and the other spouse is under 62 years of age.

Can a Reverse Mortgage be placed on a home where not both spouses/owners are over the age of 62, yes! However, there is a caveat, and something which you both must understand the consequences of.

Normally when a couple take a Reverse Mortgage and both are 62 or over, there is no problems or issues. Both are on title, both are on the mortgage loan, and both are protected under the rules and guidelines of the FHA for the HECM Reverse Mortgage.

However, when one spouse is under the age of 62, only one spouse becomes the "borrower" which means that is the only one spouse on title, and the only one on the mortgage documents, and therefore the only spouse protected under the rules and guidelines of the FHA for that Reverse Mortgage.

Therefore, a Non-Borrowing Spouse is a spouse which will not have the benefits of the Reverse Mortgage as the borrower will.

After 2014 when guidelines where changed to protect the Non-Borrowing Spouses went into effect many spouses thought they were automatically included in the mortgage and were given protection when the main borrower passed or permanently vacated the home. But this is not the case.

The FHA came up with two categories of spouses: Qualified or Eligible Non-Borrowing Spouse, and Ineligible Non Borrowing Spouse. Confusing? Read on to really be confused.

Qualified or Eligible Non-Borrowing Spouses are spouses who were married to the borrower at the time the Reverse Mortgage was taken out and continues to be married to the borrower throughout the life of the loan. In addition, they must occupy the residence with the borrower and continue so for the life of the loan. And they are protected by the due and payable deferral provisions of the loan.

The Ineligible Non-Borrowing Spouse does not occupy the property at time the loan is taken out. They are not protected under the due and payable deferral provisions of the loan. And have no benefits under the HECM loan provisions.

Now, what is the Due and Payable Deferral Provisions of the Reverse Mortgages. Many loan officers mention the remaining spouse, or the heirs have up to 12 months to decide to keep or sell a home after the death of the last borrower. Although this is true, there is a caveat which must be understood. A spouse or heir must come into ownership of the property within 90 days of the death of the last borrower. This is the key, and in many jurisdictions, the 90 days is an impossibility to achieve because it may take longer than that to go through the Courts, and Probate to get legal status on a property. So, be forewarned, and look into this issue with an Attorney to see what remedies you may have to get on title within that 90 day period.

Also, keep in mind that under the deferral period the non-borrowing spouse or heirs still have the responsibility to pay the taxes, homeowners' insurance, all HOA fees and maintain the property until the loan is paid off.

Again, as mentioned above, a Non-Borrowing Spouse will lose all benefits the borrower had under the provisions of the loan. This means, that if there was a Line of Credit which was not used, the Non-Borrowing Spouse cannot access those monies. They will not have access to the Line of Credit, any Tenure payments, or any Term payments after the death of the borrower, or when the borrower vacates the premises permanently.

Also, I strongly suggest anyone looking to take out a HECM Reverse Mortgage and has a spouse which is under the age of 62 to consult with a knowledgeable Attorney as to the best way to proceed.

Elder Abuse and Elder Financial Abuse

Elder Abuse, or Financial Exploitation is the unauthorized or illegal use of a senior adult's resources or funds for the benefit of someone else other than the senior adult. Elder abuse includes theft, fraud, or acts of deception to get control of a senior's cash, assets, belongings, or property.

Elder Abuse is perpetrated by strangers, family members, through scam schemes, through telemarketing and internet fraud tactics, by investment schemes, and through deceiving tactics which confuse older adults into making unwarranted, unjustifiable and unnecessary decisions.

Although there are many resources available to all senior adults to protect their rights and their financial assets, many do not report any abuse issues because they are intimidated, and mostly because they are embarrassed to admit they have done something wrong or that they have been taken advantage of.

We must all be cognitive of the facts surrounding our Senior population, whether they are our family member, our neighbors, or just someone who you deal with in the course of your daily life. Unfortunately, there are too many people trying to take advantage and scam our Senior members of our community, and we all must share in the responsibility to care for them all.

Elder financial abuse, also known as financial exploitation, is the illegal or unauthorized use of an older adult's funds or resources for the benefit of someone other than the older adult. This includes fraud, theft, and acts of deception to gain control over a senior's money or property.

What are some of the Signs?

Here are some of the indicators of Elder Abuse, but keep in mind that no single indicator can be taken as conclusive proof. Rather, one should look for a pattern or a collection of indicators that suggest abuse has taken place.

- Unpaid bills, eviction notices, or notices to discontinue utilities
- Withdrawals from bank accounts or transfers between accounts that the older person cannot explain

- Bank statements and canceled checks no longer come to the elder's home
- New "best friends"
- Legal documents, such as powers of attorney, which the older person didn't understand at the time he or she signed them
- Unusual activity in the older person's bank accounts including large, unexplained withdrawals, frequent transfers between accounts, or ATM withdrawals
- The care of the elder is not commensurate with the size of his/her estate
- A caregiver expresses excessive interest in the amount of money being spent on the older person
- Belongings or property are missing
- Suspicious signatures on checks or other documents
- Absence of documentation about financial arrangements
- Implausible explanations given about the elderly person's finances by the elder or the caregiver
- The elder is unaware of or does not understand financial arrangements that have been made for him or her

What to do: Report it!

If the immediate situation is threatening or dangerous call 911

Here are some places and phone numbers to contact if you suspect any form of Elder Abuse or Financial Exploitation taking place against a Senior member of your community:

National Center on Elder Abuse

800-677-1116

State by State directory of reporting numbers, government agencies, state laws, state-specific data and statistics, and other resources

https://ncea.acl.gov/resources/state.html

Consumer Fraud and Identity Theft

Contact the Federal Trade Commission at 1-877-FTC-HELP, 1-877-ID-THEFT, or online at www.ftc.gov.

US Senate Special Committee on Aging

To report scams, receive information on how to avoid/recover from scams or get referrals for other agencies, including the Better Business Bureau, you can contact the Committee's toll-free Fraud Hotline at 1-855-303-9470.

General Fraud and Other Criminal Matters

Contact the FBI at (202) 324-3000, or online at www.fbi.gov or https://tips.fbi.gov.

Health Care Fraud, Medicare/Medicaid Fraud, and Related Matters

Contact the Department of Health and Human Services, Office of the Inspector General at 1-800-HHS-TIPS, or online at www.oig.hhs.gov.

Internet Fraud and Lottery/Sweepstakes Fraud by Internet

Contact the Internet Crime Complaint Center (IC3) online at www.ic3.gov.

Mail Fraud and Lottery/Sweepstakes Fraud

Contact the U.S. Postal Inspection Service at 1-800-372-8347, or online at https://postalinspectors.uspis.gov.

Securities Fraud

Contact the Securities and Exchange Commission at 1-800-SEC-0330, by email at enforcement@sec.gov (link sends e-mail), or online at www.sec.gov.

Identity Theft and Credit Card Fraud

Gaining access to a senior's personal information to take money and property. Includes tax ID theft where a scammer uses a senior's Social Security number to file a tax return and steal the refund, or impersonates the IRS and tells the senior that the IRS is owed money.

Grandparent Scam

Pretending to be a grandchild in trouble in order to convince the senior to wire money or send prepaid debit cards.

Sweepstakes and Lottery Scams

A widely practiced form of telemarketing fraud, scammers tell seniors that they have won a lottery or sweepstakes. The catch is, the senior must make a small payment or pay a fee to receive the alleged prize. Seniors may also receive a fake check back from the scammer, which will "bounce" after it gets deposited.

Investment Schemes & Fraud

Unscrupulous professional investors try to sell inappropriate, unethical, or confusing investment products to seniors, or from con artists claiming to be the "Nigerian prince" or some other wealthy foreigner who asks for your bank account number to transfer millions of dollars into your banking account.

Healthcare Scams

Getting information about a senior's medical accounts — like Medicare and Medicaid—in order to make fraudulent claims and take advantage of these taxpayer programs.

Remember, See something...Say Something! One day you will be a Senior too.

(This information is adapted from the [Women's Institute for a Secure Retirement](#) and the [National Adult Protective Services Association](#))

Seniors vs Adult Children.

This is a very difficult topic to discuss, but it is one which must be brought up, and I can only explain it by giving a couple of examples of what I have experienced in the past 12 years of dealing with Seniors and their families. Some of what I will say here may offend some readers, but it is the truth. It may also not apply to you or your family, so I give you my disclaimer here, but it is a real factor for some other readers.

Statistics show there are 10,000 Seniors turning 65 years of age every single day in the United States! Also, many of these seniors have a life expectancy of 10, 20, even 30 years or more. This means many will live into their 80's and 90's. And, as I have said in another chapter, many desires to live in their own homes for as long as they can. What this means is they must do with whatever income they have from different sources such as social security, pensions, 401k, IRA, Investment accounts, savings, and even part time jobs. For many of these Seniors, that may not be enough. Remember they grew up when gasoline was 36 cents a gallon, bread was 25 cents a loaf, going out to dinner cost under $3.00. Prices have risen over the years faster than they have been able to save it, yet they have accomplished a great deal with the resources they had back then. For many seniors, they run out of money before the end of each month when they receive their new income check for the next month, so many are playing catch up every month.

Many Seniors I have worked with over the years have turned to the Reverse Mortgage Program from the FHA in order to supplement their income, and to have enough money to better their lives in retirement.

Yet, many of their adult children have resented their parents for taking this step to tap into the equity in their homes for money to live on. Why, have so many adult children have been against their parents using the reverse mortgage program? The most prevalent excuse I hear is that the parents are using up their equity and therefore leaving a smaller inheritance to the adult children. As difficult as it is for me to put this into words, that is exactly what I have been told over and over again by the adult children, and also the main reason for these same children to talk their parents out of taking out this loan which would help them through their financial situations for the rest of their lives.

I will never forget an 85 year old man, who had arthritis in all his fingers, and was a barber by trade, and still had to work 5 days a week to make enough money to pay for his forward mortgage payment each month, and his son in law sat down with them, and told me that "he" did not want the seniors to take the reverse mortgage because "he" would receive less money when he died. The gall! But he said it in front of them, and I was flabbergasted by his actions. The son in law said he would help them make the payments on the mortgage since he was living in the house with their daughter. Yet, after a few months, I saw the senior again, and he told me the guy had not made any payments, nor given him any money for the mortgage. What a surprise! And, how sad! But this is typical of what goes through in many families when adult children have control of the Seniors. Is this elder abuse? Not under the law, but it should be!

For those who are adult children of Seniors, I employ you, if you have the financial means to support your parents, do so. If you have the room to take them in and care for them, do so. If you do not want them living with you, or do not have the means to care for them financially, do not make the decision for them not to seek out any means available to them for financial assistance which would make their lives much easier in their retirement years. But, by all means, do not deprive them of a happy retirement just because you are more interested in your inheritance than in them. Your parents should come first, as well as their happiness, and their financial stability.

Can a Reverse Mortgage be Foreclosed?

This is an issue which comes up at every Reverse Mortgage informational meeting we have with our customers. They have heard horror stories about this scenario, and always want to know if and how this is possible on a loan which does not require any mortgage payments.

Well, the answer is quite simple: Yes, a Reverse Mortgage can be Foreclosed! But why? That is the question which must be explained and understood by all Senior borrowers. So, I will explain both the why and the how here.

Why, is a Reverse Mortgage Foreclosed. One reason is that all the Borrowers have moved out of the home. Remember, with a Reverse Mortgage, at least one Borrower must occupy the premises. If they both move away, go into nursing facility, or pass; they are no longer living in the property and therefore the loan is in default and it can be Foreclosed.

Another reason, and the one most commonly faced, is that the Borrowers fail to make their Property Tax payments each year, and the property goes into default with the County the property is in. See, the County charges every property owner a tax each year, and they want to be paid. If a Senior forgets to make these payments, they are in default, and the County has a legal right to Foreclose in order to recover those unpaid taxes owed them. However, when the County starts a Foreclosure action against a homeowner for non-payment of property taxes, the Bank must join in that Foreclosure action in order to preserve their standing in the Foreclosure, and not lose their right to recover the mortgage balance owed the Bank. This is usually what you hear in the news. So, when you hear the Bank Foreclosed on Grandma, and they kicked out into the street, it may really be the County which started the Foreclosure and not the Bank. The same goes if the Borrowers fail to make a Homeowner's Association payment, which can become a lien against the property and they also have the right to Foreclose on that property to recover the dues owed them. Lastly, there is the Homeowners Insurance which is also required to have on every property with a Reverse Mortgage. In this case, if the borrower fails to make the payments, the Bank has the right to place their own Insurance Policy on the property and bill the owners for it through the servicing statement balance.

Another reason for a Foreclosure is if the balance of the mortgage is greater than the value of the home, the Non-Recourse clause in the mortgage kicks in and the Heirs may not want to deal with this scenario, so they just turn the house over to the Bank. Since the Heirs will not get any money from the sale of the property, they have the right to turn the house over to the Bank. In this case, the Bank has the responsibility to foreclose on the loan so they can legally gain marketable title to the home in order to sell it and get it off their books. By the way: This is called a Deed In lieu of Foreclosure. But in this case, the media reports it as a "foreclosure" and gives the Program a bad name even though they are actually helping the Heirs in this case.

So, when you hear these horror stories about the Bank Foreclosing on a property which has a Reverse Mortgage on it, please check the facts and look to see the reason for the foreclosure. Most likely it will be for a legitimate reason, and not because the Banks wants to get rid of the

Senior homeowner or because they failed to make a mortgage payment (which is not required).

Although I personally do not like the fact the term "foreclosure" is used in these cases, there is nothing we in the Industry can do about it since the Federal Government does not address this issue as they do not see it as very detrimental. I guess because it does not affect them.

Today, the term "Foreclosure" is the only method by which banks have to recover a property they have a loan on which is in default. So. whether it is initiated by the County, an HOA, or other entity, the Bank must join in the suit to recover their loan balance owed them thus protecting their lien position. Also, know that when all the borrowers have moved out of the property, the loan is technically in default and the Bank does have the legal right to recover the loan balance, and that is through a Foreclosure.

I hope this point is a bit clearer to all the readers, and the next time you hear a Bank foreclosing on a reverse mortgage, or the bank threw out Grandma into the street, you will know the real reason why.

Gray Divorce and Seniors

Gray Divorce is a term used today to describe a divorce for Senior couples. Divorcing in our Senior years of life is nothing new. This has always been around, but the numbers have been very small in prior generations, but now in today's society it has become more common than you might think. For example: Government data shows that 10 out of every 1000 married couples age 50 and older divorced in 2015; compared to 5 out of 1000 in 1990.

Wow, how we have changed as a society!

What happens to a Senior couple in case of a divorce? Let me start by saying that a split late in life affects both parties in issues such as Pensions, Savings, Investments, Retirement Plans, the home, family heirlooms, children's inheritances, and personal assets. Not an easy task to divvy up, but then again, Lawyers love these kinds of challenges.

One of the largest and most battled over asset is the "marital home", because usually both parties want that home to live in. And, because neither wants to move. And, also neither wishes to give up that home they both lived in during their marriage.

As I see it there are three alternatives when dealing with a home.

One: is to sell it, divide the proceeds, and continue with your lives.

Two: is to keep it jointly, which usually opens up a can of worms.

And, third: buy out one spouse.

Here is where the dilemma starts for the Attorney, but we in the mortgage industry have come up with a potentially useful solution to this dilemma which Attorneys have been praising because it alleviates the most difficult decision which a Senior married couple must make when divorcing: The house!

One alternative is to just sell the house, split the profits, and each spouse goes on their own way.

Another alternative is by using the HECM Reverse Mortgage Program, which allows one spouse (let's say the wife in our example) to remain in the property, and take out some of the equity in the home, give it to the husband, thus allowing the husband to use those proceeds as a down payment to purchase his own property, using his own Reverse Mortgage for Purchase loan.

Let's take a close look at each situation: First, the wife will not have to make any mortgage payments in her Reverse Mortgage loan for as long as she lives in her property. By giving the proceeds to the husband, he is now able to put this money down on his own new home, and purchase his own house also using a Reverse for Purchase loan. Now, he also has his own home without having a mortgage payment on this house as long as he lives in it. Have we not just solved everyone's problems?

Those in the financial arena who have advocated for the HECM as a retirement-planning tool, have said we must emphasize the importance of working together between all the advisors in the mix such as the Attorney, the Accountants, the Financial Planners, and us, the Reverse Mortgage specialists. Together, we can make sure the needs of all our clients are met and dealt with in an amicable, equitable and professional way. There are no winners in divorce, but since this is the path many Seniors take, then we should be ready to make it as easy as possible for them to navigate through.

Line of Credit Growth Factor & it's Benefits.

One of the most misunderstood benefits of a Reverse Mortgage, is this Line of Credit Growth!

HELOC's

We all know basically how a Home Equity Line of Credit or HELOC works from any Bank, right. Heloc's are a line of credit a bank gives a homeowner from which they can draw from until they reach the maximum allowed credit line. The homeowner then pays the bank a fee each month for the amount they have drawn and used until it is paid back to the Bank.

In most cases the Heloc is made for a period of 10 years the homeowner can draw the funds from, and after the end of the first 10 years, it becomes a 20 year loan self-amortized, which means it carries a set dollar payment each month for the next 20 years.

In addition, the Bank retains the right to cancel your line of credit any time they chose to, and for any reason. They can also freeze your line of credit at will and require you to start making amortized payments from that point on.

And, to make matters worse, your Heloc line of credit can does not increase in value as time goes by. And, you make payments when required in order to lower the loan balance. And, yes, all Heloc's are Mortgages on your property. This is also a misunderstanding by most borrowers. When asked if they have one or two mortgages, they usually omit the Heloc because they feel a Line of Credit is not a Mortgage, wrong, they are!

Reverse Mortgage Credit Line:

Now, a Reverse Mortgage Line of Credit is a bit different. Here the Federal Government is the one guaranteeing your Line of Credit. It is also attached to the interest rate on your original loan, which represents the Credit Line Growth factor each year.

First, this Credit Line cannot be frozen by the Bank or by the Government. It is a contractual obligation they signed with you when you took out the Reverse Mortgage, and it is in effect for as long as you retain the Reverse Mortgage loan. The Line of Credit also cannot be taken away from you because of economic changes.

Second, if you look at your stated interest rate each year, that is exactly the same as the growth factor of this Line of Credit. So, the money you have in the Reverse Mortgage Line of Credit will grow each year by the same factor as your interest rate stated on your loan. Read this carefully, because it is most important, and it is quite often misunderstood. Many Financial Planners and Advisors today are seeing the valuable benefit of this Credit Line Growth and suggesting to their investors to use this feature for the growth of their Line of Credit even if they do not need the funds today. In the future, they may need it, and it is there for them.

How to Help Elder Parents.

There have been many reports conducted by many Companies that have estimated the costs involved for adult children who take care of their elderly parent or parents. One such report conducted by Met Life estimated the cost to the economy is almost $3 trillion. And for individuals who provide daily caregiving the average cost is a staggering $324,000.

Nothing that I can writer will make it any easier for you, the adult children, or for your parents to be able to deal with this fact the parents are going to get older. But, what to do?

Now is the time to talk to everybody about this topic. Get both parents, brothers, sisters, uncles, aunts, and anyone else who loves your parents to talk about what will be done when the parents can no longer take care of themselves. Not an easy topic, but certainly one which should be discussed because both the mental and financial burden may be reduced if it is shared by all.

Start by who will care for them. Will it be a family member? Will it be an outside organization? Will it be a local neighborhood person who knows them and will take on this task for a fee? The thing to do is to start before they need full time care and start by having a cleaning lady or housekeeper stop by once a month, so they can start to know them and trust them. Over time, that person may take on more duties.

What are your parents' payments options? One shortcoming is that most of us do not carry Long Term Insurance. Medicare does not cover Long Term Care either. So, in most cases this is a cost borne by the family. Long Term Care Insurance is right behind life insurance as a priority by most young adults, and cost prohibitive for most parents. There are some programs out there that combine life insurance with Long Term Care Insurance, and although they are not cheap, they can be converted if the need arose in the future.

When looking at Long Term Care Insurance, be careful as to the amount it will pay out on a daily basis, and also the total number of days the coverage will last. No two programs are alike, and no two will cost the same. Consult a professional on the costs and coverages, and by all means start early to discuss the alternatives available with all family members before they are no longer alternatives.

So, you want to leave your home to your kids?

I have heard these words often enough throughout my mortgage career, and also on a personal level from my own mother. Yes, my mother told me these words back in 2000 when she owned a home, with a small $35,000 mortgage on it, and the house was worth about $300,000; but, no she did not want to take out a reverse mortgage because, well, she did not understand it, and she thought I would not get anything from it when she passed. So, she wanted to leave me the house, but here's what she, and most of us do not accept; she lived in this house for the past 45 years, she had done little upgrading to the house over those years. I asked her when was the last time she re-did the roof? When had she replaced the water heater? When was the electrical system updated? When had she replaced the washer and dryer? (okay, this was replaced 14 years earlier). The carpeting was also replaced some 9 years ago. The stove and refrigerator were the originals from when she bought the house. Are you seeing a pattern here? Most of the stuff in the house was 45 years old.

So, I asked her why did she want to leave me a 45 year old problem ready to explode on me?

I would bet that many of your kids will feel the same way about your homes. In fact, ask them! I would also bet that most of your kids will tell you they will not want to live in your home. This is a fact you must learn to deal with. Our kids do not want our homes because they have their own homes to live in. Of course, there will always be those few who do want your home, and will live in it because they do not have anywhere else to live. To those, I tip my hat to you, and say this is not a program for you.

However, for those of you who know your kids only want your house for the money, you know who they are, and that they will sell it as soon as you pass and take the money and run. Or, for those of you who know your kids could use the money to live on and must sell your house to get the necessary cash to deal with their own lives; I have a possible solution for you. But first, let me state that the point I wish to get across to all of you, is that this is about YOU, not your kids!

There is still a lot of life in you, and you should get yourself a "bucket list" of things you want to accomplish while you are still living. The rest of your life is about YOU, and no one else. One of the hardest things in life is to budget your money so you can do the things you want to do in life and have enough of it, so you do not run out of money. This is why many of us go through life not doing what we want in fear of running out of cash to live on. This is where the reverse mortgage comes in. Yes, it has been changed over the past few years to protect the Seniors who chose this Government guaranteed program to take some of the equity in their homes and turn it into cash they can spend on themselves and on thing they want to do in life.

Now, let's take a look at some of the most common things we chose to do to leave the house to our kids. Many Seniors, it has been established, have no mortgage, or a small one on their homes. Many homes are 20 years or older. Many homes need upgrading. And for a large majority of us, we have about $100,000 to $200,000 in equity to leave to our heirs.

Let's take a look at how this works when you pass. You could have your house in a Trust, that is very good. Or you could have a Will designating the house to go to your kids, this is better than nothing. Yet, many of the Seniors I have encountered do not have either, and they think it's an automatic the kids get the house, not true, the State may get your house. So you need to do some questioning and get answers, consult with a legal professional before it's too late.

Say you have the house in a Trust, when you pass, the beneficiaries of your Trust will receive title to the house, as I said this is good. It's a fast process, the kids get the house, and they can sell it right away. If you have a Will, as many of us do, you may think your kids will get the house automatically, hold the phone here, it must first go through "probate". This is a nasty word because they will most likely need an Attorney (a cost), then go through the Court system which may take 6 months to a year for the kids to get title on the house before they can sell it (more costs). And, then there are those who do not have a Will, and the heirs must go to Court first to prove they are the heirs, and they have a right to the house. (another big cost). This is called dying "intestate". Where do you stand? And as I always caution everyone, seek the legal advice of an Attorney to get the facts straight, don't just take my word here, I'm not an Attorney.

So, now you should know where you stand with the house, but you still have the dilemma of wanting to leave the money to your kids as well as wanting to enjoy your life and do some things which you never got to do, and this costs money. This is where the FHA's Reverse Mortgage Program comes in. Well why not look into it, you just may be surprised like many Attorneys and Financial Planners have, that this is a great program the Government has come up with so

Seniors can remain in their homes, have extra cash to live on, and enjoy their lives.

One thing I love about the Program is the security it offers a senior couple that when one passes, nothing happens to the other one, or to the house, or to the mortgage. There is still no payment required form the remaining spouse, however, that spouse may stay in the house with no mortgage payments due. Another issue is that if the equity in your home increases over time, you can refinance a Reverse Mortgage and get more cash out of the house in later years. Also, if you decide in any future year that you had enough of this house and wish to move to another home, or another State, you can do so, and purchase a new home using a Reverse Mortgage (qualifying is required) and again not have any mortgage payments to make. Above I mentioned I may have a solution for you to leave money to your kids. Well, since many of you will be getting a large sum from the reverse mortgage, why not take out a $100,000 or $200,000 10 year term life insurance policy, and name your kids as beneficiaries? The cost can be paid from the mortgage proceeds, and this way the kids will get the money right away without having to go through the probate fiasco, it will be tax free money, and you still have enough cash to enjoy your retirement and the rest of your life.

I have many other scenarios which I have dealt with throughout my career in the Reverse Mortgage and if you would like to share your situation with me, I would be glad to offer some of my expertise and experiences with you. I'll be glad to help, just contact me at: ReverseGeorge@gmail.com

Pass on Equity Before You Die

So, now you have read about Leaving the House to your Kids, now let's look at a different situation: What if you were to give some of the Inheritance you will be leaving for your kids, but while you are still alive?

I know, it is tradition to leave the house, preferably, debt free to your children. But, why? You have worked all your lives for the kids, for the house, for everything you have. What if, you had enough finances to carry you through your retirement years, why not help out your adult kids, even your grandchildren, when they may need it the most, and before you pass.

Let's say you are in your mid 60's or mid 70's; that would mean your "kids" may be in their late 30's, 40's or 50's. Wow! This is an age when they may need your inheritance money more than after you pass when they may be nearing retirement themselves. Think about it! When they are in their mid-life years is when they may be able to use that money, you are going to leave them years from now. Also, in some cases you may be able to help out your grandchildren by setting up annuities, or special accounts which will benefit them when they are older (and you are no longer around). Wow, wouldn't that be a great legacy to leave them.

So, what if you were to get a Reverse Mortgage, get some of the free equity in your home out now, and give some (just some) of that money to your kids to pay down their monthly debt, their student loans, their own mortgage, or other non-recurring debt. Remember, you will not have any mortgage payments on that Reverse Mortgage you took out, and you can do whatever you want with the proceeds, so you can gift it to your children.

Yes, they will get less from the sale of your home after you pass, but they will have that money today, when they may need it most! Think about this before you turn off your mind to the loan. It's always nice to get an inheritance, but let's be realistic, as I have said before, your kids would probably use the money today more than they would appreciate it years from now when they may be nearing their own retirement and may not have that much of a financial need for the money then.

What I talk about in this chapter are for those people who do not need a Reverse Mortgage, that have enough assets and investments or a great retirement plan, so these are the people I am addressing in this chapter. If Seniors know they have enough to live on, maybe those people should consider divesting themselves of some of their equity now before they pass.

Once I learned from a customer who came to me for a Reverse Mortgage for this exact purpose, and he taught me that what he wanted to do was to be able to give some money to his kids while he was alive so he could see what they would do with his money, and at the same time give them guidance as to what they should do with his money. The rest of their inheritance was coming to them after he passed, but for now he could control what they did with his money. I thought his was a wonderful idea, and that is why I am passing it on to all my readers.

Sandwich Generation

As reported in AARP Public Policy Institute fact sheet; "Nearly one in four (22 percent) middle aged and older workers (ages 45 to 64) — typically caring for a parent—report being family caregivers; the largest of any age group in the labor force." This responsibility puts definite strains on personal relationships; caring for children/teenagers and spouse, holding down a job, while trying to maintain a social life. This life stage is titled the Sandwich Generation!

Symptoms of relationship strain can be subtle, or not, and we may not notice until we find ourselves feeling very alone and isolated. Friends stop calling because we have no time for what seems idle chit-chat; we are too tired or busy for lunch or coffee, and our friends do not want to listen to our caregiver problems.

The children don't ask questions or tell you what happened in school because they feel you are no longer interested. Spouses try to pick up the slack, but it isn't the same as having you both involved in their life. Being a supportive, understanding spouse is hard because they are feeling neglected too. Home is not the same with no clear timeline when things will be normal again. Everyone is pulling back, and you feel lonely.

Work is a struggle, you are physically there, most of the time, but mentally and emotionally you are having a hard time focusing and keeping up with routine daily activities. Your manager is trying to be as sympathetic as possible but at times it is difficult to overlook things; such as: time spent on the phone talking about your caregiver responsibilities, being called away for emergencies or taking time off for medical appointments.

The tension palpable when you are together with your siblings. They might feel you are hogging the responsibility and do not want to share the caregiver responsibility. While you feel they are allowing you to take on all the responsibility and not offering their help.

Whatever the relationship everyone is suffering. With so many different emotions and feelings going on it is difficult to cope. Something needs to change.

Create a plan before you become a member of the Sandwich Generation! Why?

- To avoid life strains that develop with relationships when caring for parents.
- Everyone knows, understands, and agrees how things are going to be handled.
- The future is tomorrow, and changes happen in life without warning so the time to plan is now!

Have the conversations and develop a plan so every family member will be making informed decisions when the future hits you in the face. The future could be tomorrow!

Why do Reverse Mortgages Require Counseling & Forward Mortgages Don't?

This question comes up quite often, mostly because if you are a Senior, and go to any Bank to apply for a "Forward" mortgage, you do not need to go through this Counseling step.

However, the Federal Government in their infinite wisdom, wants to make positively sure that Seniors who want, and apply for a Reverse Mortgage are aware of all the facts before they actually apply for this loan. Personally, I actually believe this is the right step for the Government to take to protect our Seniors from being taken advantage of. In fact, it is my opinion that all Seniors over a certain age should be required to take this Counseling course, so  they learn not only the facts about the Reverse Mortgage Program, but also ALL the options they have as well as the consequences of obtaining a Forward mortgage and tying themselves up for another 30 year loan.

Let's face it, a person who is 65, 70, 75 or older, why would they desire to get themselves into a 30 year obligation? You must realize, pardon me here, you may very well never reach the goal of paying this loan off. And, even if you did, why would you want to burden yourself with such a monthly payment which will cut into your retirement finances and possibly cut back on what your dreams and goals are for your retirement years.

Over the years, I have seen many Seniors who have gone to their local bank to refinance their current mortgage, or get a second mortgage, or even get a Home Equity Line of Credit, and tie themselves into making another higher payment than they used to have, and for another new 15 or 30 years! Why?

As a Senior looking forward to retirement, shouldn't you be looking to free up your money? Shouldn't you be looking to have more free cash each month now that you may be living off of a fixed income?

And, also, allow me to point out a fact we seldom look at. A Senior applying for a mortgage will be required to qualify for the loan, most likely, using both spouses' income. This will include both

Social Security incomes, any pension income, any 401K income, even savings and investment incomes. However, as I have stated before in my other books, the one thing we can guarantee is that one spouse will fall ill, need special assistance, maybe a nursing facility, or even pass before the other. When this happens, and you have a "forward" mortgage, the remaining spouse must continue to make that mortgage payment each and every month even though they will lose one income!

As a Senior, do you really want to put your spouse in that spot? I have seen many widows (and widowers) who come to me after a spouse has passed, and they are about to lose their home because they can no longer make the mortgage payment. Remember, that even after a loss, the Bank will require you to continue making that payment, and if you miss 3 months, they start Foreclosure action, and you could lose your home.

Please think ahead, because with a Reverse Mortgage both spouses are protected, and the remaining spouse can stay in the home without having to make any payments as long as they want, of course as long as they pay the taxes, insurance, HOA, and maintain the property. What peace of mind could this bring to your, your spouse and your family! Also remember a spouse may want to sell the home, and move closer to other family members, and purchase a new home, and again use a Reverse Mortgage for that purchase (yes, you must qualify) but it is another positive alternative you leave your spouse, along with peace of mind!

Before any Senior applies for a "forward" mortgage and tie themselves to another monthly payment for a long period of time, I urge you all to learn about how the Reverse Mortgage can help you. I always say: "An Informed Consumer is our best Customer".

The HECM For Purchase Program for Retirees

When buying a house, most buyers have two options. They can pay cash for the house, if they have enough extra financial resources. However, most buyers choose not to use up so much of their retirement resources and opt to leverage their purchase by going to a Bank and asking for a "forward" mortgage, and in most cases be tied to a monthly payment for 30 years or more likely the rest of their lives. Today, Seniors 62 years of age and older have a third option; They can purchase the home using the FHA's HECM Reverse Mortgage for Purchase.

Let's take a quick look at each way of purchasing that same house. With, what we call a "forward" mortgage, the one we are all used to getting at any local bank, which requires the borrower to make a monthly payment each month. We are all accustomed to this idea because it is what we all grew up with. But what happens if you miss a payment or two or three, due to an illness, an accident, a spousal death, or due to a financial change in life? One, no one really worries about. Two, it becomes a bit more difficult to make up. Three missed payment, and it's extremely difficult to catch up financially. And, after the third month, the Bank will start the foreclosure process on the 91st day. What I call "the start of no return". Always, remember with a "forward" mortgage your responsibility is to make those monthly payments no matter what happens in your life, or how much money you have left in the bank or at the end of each month to live on.

The interest payments on that 30-year mortgage is easily calculated. A 30-year fixed rate mortgage at 3.5% for $240,000 (80% of the cost of a $300,000 house), if held to maturity, would entail payments totaling $387,973, of which $147,973 would be interest. However, 30 years is a long time, and how old will you be??? Will you even make that final payment?

The second option: Paying cash means that one foregoes the earnings that money might otherwise have generated for you. So, by paying cash for that $300,000 house, how much interest income will you lose because you used up all that money to have the privilege of not having a mortgage payment and the security of knowing no Bank will be able to foreclose on you?

The third option: As stated above, a home buyer who is 62 years of age and older has the option of purchasing the home using a modest down payment and a HECM Reverse Mortgage for Purchase. The HECM requires a larger down payment than a "forward" mortgage, yes, but the reverse mortgage does not require any monthly payment of while the home is the primary residence of at least one of the borrowers.

How does it work?

Using the same figures, where the purchase price is $300,000, and the borrowers are 62 years old, the HECM for Purchase Program would make available about $155,000 in a mortgage, thus having the buyers coming up with only $145,000 as a cash down payment. This figure is much smaller than buying for cash where you needed to bring in the full $300,000 as your payment, or the $147,943 in interest form the forward mortgage. In addition, you know you do not have to make any more monthly payments for as long as one of the borrowers lives in the home. What a relief this will be when you consider this benefit. Think about it for a few minutes. Being able to live in your home without having to make any more mortgage payments and being able to sell the home if at a future date you wish to move somewhere else, and purchase there with another reverse mortgage! Wow, still thinking about it.

One more thing. If you take the reverse mortgage out, you have that extra cash you would have sent to the Bank each month, remember that mortgage payment amount, to spend on yourselves. You have this money each month to live out a more active lifestyle. You can use this money to make your retirement years more meaningful by traveling, spending on your family, on yourself, or for things which you may not have been able to afford if you were sending this amount to the bank every month!

Which of these three options would you think is the best one? Only way to be sure, is to look into the Program more carefully, educate yourself by discussing it with a Professional, and making the first move.

What Happens After the Death; What Heirs & Family Must Know.

Many erroneous articles have been written about what happens to a property which has a Reverse Mortgage and all the borrowers have passed away. Part of these erroneous believes stem from the fact that not many people understand the Reverse Mortgage Loans themselves. It is widely believed that when a person takes out a Reverse Mortgage on their home, the Bank own the home. This is not true! People believe when they have a Reverse Mortgage, I guess because they have not had to make any monthly payments, that the Bank will inherit the home. This is also not true!

In fact, a Reverse Mortgage is just like any other mortgage you may have had on your property! It's just a "mortgage". In fact, when you check out the County Records you will never see the word "Reverse" on any document recorded. Why? Because it's just a mortgage and like with any type of mortgage that debt must be paid off at some point.

So, let's look at a "forward" mortgage situation. Your parents take out a "forward" mortgage with any Bank and take a 30 year term. After 20 years, both borrowers pass away, you (their child) inherit the property via their Will, what do you do? You, the "child" inherits the house, and after Probate, the title passes to your name. However, the original mortgage your parents took out 20 years ago, is still in their names. So, this debt, their debt, must be paid off by you taking out a new mortgage in your own name. Now, the house belongs to you, and the new mortgage is in your name.

Well, with a Reverse Mortgage the process is exactly the same as with any regular mortgage!

So, if this process is the same, as in the "forward" world of lending, why has the Reverse Mortgage Program received such a negative reputation? It has mainly to do with the lack of education on the program, the lack of understanding of the type of loan it is, and the lack of professional information one receives in the marketplace. Many of my customers have told me that in many cases they had heard negative information from their friend, old drinking buddies, even other family members. I have asked them, if they had a medical illness would they seek the advice of their landscaper? Or if they had a legal situation, would they ask their Aunt Mary? Or, even if they wanted to borrow money would they go to their Doctor for advice? Yet, this is what we have done with the Reverse Mortgage Product. We as a society have gone to non-professionals and sought their advice for something which they know little about, it's just hearsay, and, then swore this to be the truth and correct for all time!

Let's take a look at what actually happens when all the borrowers of a property secured with a Reverse Mortgage passes away.

There are basically two options for handling any mortgage, even a reverse mortgage after the death of the borrowers.
- Sell the Property.
- Keep the Property.

Most children of Seniors do not have a need or desire to live in the house their parents lived in. In most cases, the children are already grown adults, who have their own families, and their own homes with their own mortgages. So, when inheriting their parent's home, they have a need to see it and pocket the money from that sale. As I stated above, no matter what kind of mortgage was on the parent's house, that debt must get paid off first, the remaining balance goes to the children.

In a case of the house having a Reverse Mortgage, the process is the same. The house can be sold, the mortgage paid off, and the balance of the money goes to the children. Easy, nothing new, nothing drastic to learn or overcome.

In those cases where a child of a senior inherits the house, and they wish to keep it, as a rental or to live in it themselves, the same holds true for the underlying mortgage. Once the title is transferred to the child, they have the obligation to pay off their parent's mortgage and take one out in their own names. This is where the law gets a bit muddy. It is the believe of many children that when they inherit a property with a forward loan from their parents, they can just continue to make the payments on that "forward" loan, and not have to change the name of the borrowers on that loan. This is not the case! As mentioned before, both the title and the mortgage must be in the same name. There have been many cases where the inheriting child cannot qualify for their own mortgage, and they try to do nothing in the hopes the bank does not find out their parents are gone, and they are now living in that home. They will find out! The same holds true for a property with a Reverse Mortgage. Once the parents are not living in the property the loan is due, and there is an obligation to pay this balance off either by selling the property or by refinancing it in the names of the new owners (the children).

What if you are the Spouse of a deceased borrower?

When one spouse passes, and the surviving spouse is a borrower on the reverse mortgage, nothing happens. The terms of the loan remain the same and the surviving spouse retains all the benefits of the loan.

However, if the surviving spouse is not a borrower, that surviving spouse may not have the same rights under the loan terms as the borrower had. One must check with the Servicer in order to determine the actual rights of the surviving spouse under the loan agreement. The Servicer will send a letter stating the requirements for the deferral period before the loan is due and payable. When the spouse receives this notice, they may choose to sell the home, keep the home by paying off the reverse mortgage loan amount due, or by a deed in lieu which gives the Title of the property to the lender.

Keep in mind that during the deferral period, the property must be maintained, the property taxes paid, and the homeowner's insurance must be kept in force.

All surviving spouses should communicate with the loan Servicer to obtain all the rights available to that spouse.

What if the Heirs responsibility for the Reverse Mortgage after the death of all the Borrowers?

When the last borrower passes, the heirs will receive a notice from the Servicer with information on the borrower's estate, details of the reverse mortgage agreement, and all available options the heirs have in order to satisfy the loan. It is the responsibility of the heirs to inform the Servicer with whether they wish to keep the property, sell it, or do the deed in lieu back to the Bank.

If the heirs wish to keep the property, the Servicer will have an appraisal done, and their cost to pay off the reverse mortgage will be 95% of that appraised value. This is so even if the balance on the loan is greater than the value of the house. Keep in mind that the reverse mortgage has a non-recourse clause in it, which states the heirs will not be responsible for any loan balance greater than the value of the house. However, if the value is greater than the loan balance, they can sell the house, the reverse mortgage is paid off, and the heirs get to keep the difference.

What if you are a non-borrower and are still living in the property?

Sometimes there are adult children living in the same property as Seniors who have taken out a reverse mortgage and when all the borrowers on the loan passes, then the remaining adult children are faced with a situation in which the loan will become due and payable by them, as the heirs of the borrowers. It is imperative for all who live in the same house as the reverse mortgage borrowers understand their responsibility when they inherit a property.

Let's look at the legal implications of any mortgage (forward or reverse) loan on a property. When there is a mortgage on a property, the names on the mortgage must be the same as the names on the deed on that property. Many of us don't realize this fact. So, when there is a mortgage in the names of, say the parents, and they pass, the children inherit the house, but hat mortgage must also be changed into the names of the children inheriting it. How this is done, is a legal matter which all heir must look into and be familiar with before this becomes an issue after the death of the parents. See an attorney for this information.

What is the timeline.

The Government will give the heirs of a property with a Reverse Mortgage up to 6 months to determine what they want to do with that property and to satisfy that debt. The heirs may also request two additional 3 month extensions which must be requested from HUD before the time expires on the previous timeline. Be careful here, this is where many people get confused thinking it is an automatic extension. It must be requested and approved before you are granted the extra time extensions.

Within 30 days of receiving notice of the death of the last borrower the Loan Servicer will send out a due and payable notice to the Estate along with information on the balance of the reverse loan and the eligibility requirements for an extension period if needed on the reverse mortgage.

The heirs have up to 6 months to sell the property, and they may request up to two 3 month extensions from the FHA in order to finalize the sale of the property. But, remember these 90 day extensions must be requested before the previous one expires. And, it is up to HUD's approval, they are not automatic extensions.

The heirs must also respond to all correspondence from the Servicer and to all due and payable notices they receive, otherwise the Servicer may start foreclosure action. In addition, if the taxes are not paid on time, the homeowner's insurance is in place, or the time extensions expire, the Servicer also has the right to start a foreclosure action on the property. So, I recommend all heirs to work closely with the Servicer to avoid any foreclosure action on their part.

Estate Planning Issues for People with Pets.

Does anyone else remember reading "Rhubarb," a 1946 novel by H. Allen Smith? The basic story: an eccentric millionaire leaves his entire fortune to a stray cat (the eponymous Rhubarb). Among the assets in the cat's inheritance is a baseball team (the fictional New York Loons). Hilarity ensues. The novel was even made into a movie in 1951. My story is about my three dogs, not cats, but it's the same outcome.

Why does this all-but-forgotten novel (and the movie, which may actually be better than the book) come to mind now? Because of the growing popularity of "pet trusts," and as an opportunity to discuss how one might plan for taking care of the pets who survive the owner's death.

So, you have two dogs (Lucky and Dukey) and a dog (Ginger), and you feel very strongly about them. You want to make sure that they are taken care of after your death -- even though you recognize that you will likely outlive them. In any case, you would almost certainly have other pets, and you know that they will be very important to you when you are looking at the proverbial endgame. What can you do to provide for Lucky, Dukey and Ginger, and what *should* you do?

There are a number of mechanisms our clients consider for dealing with their pets. In roughly increasing order of complexity, they include:

Identifying who will take custody of the pets. Probably the most common arrangement we see is something like this: "I direct that any pets I may own at the time of my death should be given to my brother Mike, who has promised that he will care for them." Please make sure Mike knows he is identified in this way, and you probably should have an alternate choice

Involving a pet-oriented non-profit. Some organizations offer placement programs for pets after the owner's death. You might want to make specific reference to a program you are familiar with and include a donation to allow the organization to effectively make a placement for an elderly, ill or special-needs pet (remember that your pet's condition is likely to decline between now and your death).

Providing for a stipend. We frequently see one of two variations here. Either "I leave the sum of $x,000 to my sister Linda, on condition that she takes custody of all of my pets and agrees to care for them" or "I leave the sum of $x,000 to my veterinarian Dr. Healer, who has agreed to use some or all of those funds to help arrange for placement of my beloved Lucky, Dukey and Ginger (and any other pets I may own at the time of my death) in suitable homes." Again, make sure your intended recipient is aware of the arrangement and willing to take it on, and plan for a backup (Dr. W is planning on selling his veterinary practice within the next five years, you know).

Making more elaborate arrangements for pets. Occasionally we have clients who have given a lot of thought to what their pets' lives will look like after the client's death. We have drafted a number of specific arrangements, from giving directions about the kind of care (food, grooming, living arrangements) to providing a home for the person who keeps the pets. These arrangements do not quite rise to the next level of complexity, since they are not formal "pet trusts" -- but they can be as tailor-made and as complicated as the client's needs and imagination.

Pet trusts. This is a topic of considerable interest in recent years, though it has been (in our experience) much more talked about than implemented. Pet trusts have actually been around for centuries (look for the legal term "honorary trusts"), but local laws have often made them unenforceable. In the last two decades or so, many jurisdictions have formally approved the idea: Rhubarb would be proud.

But a pet trust is a much more complicated and expensive thing to create -- and administer -- than the other, less formal arrangements. For that reason, most of our clients, though they may be intrigued by the idea, opt instead to use one of the more casual approaches described above. That said, if you feel strongly that care of your pet is one of the most important items your estate plan needs to consider, you should be thinking about a pet trust.

Can you get a pet trust on the internet? After all, your situation can not be unique -- millions of people with beloved pets must be thinking about the same thing. Our answer: yes, you can get a straightforward pet trust from the internet, and it will probably be legal in most States. But it will not be integrated into your estate plan and might in fact directly conflict. It may affect the other distributions you intend to make. If your pet is going to be your sole beneficiary it might work better -- but then there are the problems of trust administration, and your pet's trustee will probably end up paying more in legal fees than if you developed a relationship with a lawyer during your life (and customized your pet's trust to the terms you really want to cover).

What about the possibility that Ginger, Lucky and Dukey might not survive you? Whatever arrangements you make for pets should probably be generic -- rather than providing for those three pets by name, you probably want to include *any* pets you might have at death. And don't forget: your pet desert tortoise and parrot might very well outlive you -- and they therefore might require more careful planning.

One thing, let the person who will be taking care of the pets know about their job, and let the person who will be handling the rest of your estate know, too. Immediate care of your pets is **one of the most important things your family will need to deal with** upon your death or incapacity.

You get more information? <u>from the Humane Society</u> of the United States.

Senior with Pets, What to do?

In today's world many Seniors have pets, which are regarded as a family member. In most cases, these four legged family members have been with them for 4, 7, even 10 years or longer. These pets are not only a family member, but they are a daily companion to the Seniors, especially after the passing of one spouse. In many cases, these pets are closer to the Senior than their actual two-legged family members.

But, what happens to these pets when all the Seniors pass, or have to move into an Assisted Living or Nursing Home?

Will their family members take care of the Seniors' pets?

Will someone be in charge of finding the pet a new home?

Let me share a personal experience. My mother had a dog named Lucky who was 7 years old when she passed. She used to ask me, "who will take care of your brother when I die?" Well, Lucky was my only "brother" since I was an only child, but what she asked was a turning point for me because I was not sure what would happen to him. Of course, she told me to take care of the dog, and find him a good home. And, I wanted to do the right things and care for "my brother" but he was 2000 miles away from my home.

How was I going to care for him? Well, I had my own family, had my own dog (Dukey), and we certainly did not need another pet in the house. However, this situation is what led me to investigate and develop the information I will share here with you. By the way, I did do the right thing by Lucky, you will see!

My research led me to some questions which needed more research and to establish a method of sharing this information with other Seniors.

Questions like:
What will happen to the pets if a Senior cannot care for them anymore?

What options are available for arranging for the future care of a pet?

What kind of steps need to be taken in case of a pet's emergency care?

Can a Senior designate a caregiver and/or a guardian for a pet?

Can a pet be included into a person's Will?

What is a Pet Trust?

Can a Senior leave money set aside for the care of a pet?

What will happen to a pet if the family does not wish to care for them?

And this is just the tip of the iceberg. There so many questions that it will be impossible to answer them all in this chapter, but I will hit on a few of them, and leave you with a resource to find out more.

First, let's look at the most common situation of what happens to a Senior's pet when one passes. The family gathers, and they either wish to keep the pet or not to keep the pet.

If they desire to keep the pet, great, that pet will have a home and live a fruitful life with the family. But in many, many cases, the family cannot (or does not want) the pet in their homes. Many give the reason they do not want an older (7 years or older) pet. So, what do they do? Again, most common is to take the pet to a shelter. Most probably not what the Senior wanted for their "family" member. Next comes the worst-case scenario, which is they just let the pet out of the home to go wherever it goes, never to been seen again.

For me, I found a family just behind my mother's house who had just lost their dog, and since they knew my mother's dog, Lucky, they came to me and asked if they could take and care for Lucky. I was very fortunate to find a loving family for him to be with, and right behind my mother's fence, and I knew my mother would approve. A rare instance, and one which does not happen very often. See, many families do not want to care for an elderly dog or cat either. They feel the older the animal, the more expenses they will incur due to illness, or Vet bills. Also, some3 shelters, if the animal is not adopted, they may be euthanized. Again, not what the Senior would have wanted.

To some of the answers: Yes, you may include a pet into your Will. Yes, you can create a Trust for your pet. And, yes, you can designate a caregiver or guardian for your pet. Believe it or not, these are all available through Legal Zoom where you can fill out a specific form. Of course, each State may have its own laws about pet care, so you should consult a legal professional in your State for additional guidance about your pet.

Pet Trust are very similar to regular Trusts we know about, but they are specific to your pet. With them a Senior can designate how and where their pet will be cared for, they can leave funds to be used for the care of the pet, and they can even designate funeral arrangements for the pet.

The ASPCA is a great source of information to research what is available for your pet. Other sources are Pet Smart stores or their web site; ask your personal Attorney for guidance; Animal Shelters web sites; the Humane Society; and Legal Zoom. Of course, always Google, Pet Trusts.

The one thing which all agencies request is for the pet owners to create a profile with pertinent information on the pet such as food preferences, medical conditions, Veterinary information, special habits of the pet, even behavioral specifics around other animals or people.

Did you know there are "pet retirement homes"? Some are sponsored by large corporation, or universities, or veterinary associations. There are many possibilities which one should investigate to determine which is the right way to proceed for your pet's future.

Finally, do not forget the Senior, as owner of the pet has the right to establish a funeral arrangement for their pets even after the Senior has passed.

Proposed Changes for 2020

For 2020 there have been a few changes proposed which will affect the HECM Reverse Mortgage Program.

Some of these changes are Administrative which calls for the Director of the FHA to make the changes effective with merely his signature, while other changes will require Congressional Legislative approvals, which will take some time to implement. We all know how slow changes in Congress takes, so if these are to be implemented, we still have time before they actually take effect.

The main change that will affect the most Seniors is the elimination of the HECM to HECM refinance option. Yes, that means that if you currently have a Reverse Mortgage which you took out several years ago, and your property value has gone up dramatically, and you wish to refinance that HECM loan in order to take advantage of the higher property value, well, you can no longer be able to refinance that loan. This will impact older seniors who had taken out their reverse mortgage years ago. And if you take out a reverse mortgage out in 2020, that will mean that you will not be able to refinance in the future. (unless the Program changes again).

Another proposed change is the development of servicing standards for the HECM Program to reduce operational and financial burdens on servicers and the FHA. What does this mean? Simply put, it does not affect the Senior borrowers, but its aimed at the Servicers of the loan after you close. The servicers are the ones who send out the loan statements each month, and the ones you deal with when the loan is due.

Then there are the Appraisal revisions, which will be extended. This requires the need for a second appraisal to be performed in some random case in order to substantiate the value of the first appraisal done on a property. This change is a burden on all borrowers, because they do not know if and when a second appraisal will be required. And, if one is required, the lower of the two values is used to determine the amount of the loan you will get. Not fair, in my book. But "fair" is not the issue here, it is merely to cover the FHA in case of two different values. And, believe me since appraisals are an interpretation of value by a human being, they will always (99% of the time) come in at a different value. This is not an exact science! In the end, the Senior gets the short end of this stick.

Then there are a couple of Legislative Changes which require Congressional Legislative changes which will also take time to implement.

One is the elimination of National Loan Limits and return to regional loan limits. Currently all FHA HECM loans have a loan limit of $726,525, but this may change too each individual County Loan Limits. There are over 3900 Counties in the United States, and each one will have a different loan limit. And, it will be lower than the current number for sure. This will mean the loan amount a borrower will qualify for will be reduced (unless the lending factors are changed, which is unlikely) and thus the Senior, once again, will pay the price by getting less money from the Reverse Mortgage.

One more Legislative change is the proposal to separate the HECM loans from the FHA's Insurance Fund Capital Reserve account. Currently, the FHA has a fund which pays out on delinquent accounts, and it includes "forward" as well as reverse mortgages. This Funds is about

$14.5 billion in the red. And by separating the two, it will make it look "better" to the Federal Government because the numbers will be smaller. Smoke and mirrors, I say. However, this change will also not affect the Senior borrower.

Lastly, another change the FHA is implementing this year is to make it easier for Borrowers living in Condominiums which are not FHA approved, to get those properties approved so owners of these Condos could qualify for the Reverse Mortgages on their units. We must applaud the FHA for this move. We have been fighting for this one for years and it's about time we can finally help those living in Condos.

Second Appraisal Requirement

The FHA has come up with a new requirement that in some cases (and they say is on a random case) a second appraisal will be required to be done in order to verify the value of a house.

Why has this requirement come about?

Who has to pay for this second appraisal?

What effect will it have on your loan?

What alternatives does the borrower have?

Let's take a look at each issue separately. Why is a second appraisal required. The FHA has determined that many appraisal values are inflated in favor of the borrower. This would mean the borrowers would be entitled to more money from their Reverse Mortgage. And of course, this is not acceptable. Not really, that's my two cents. What they are trying to control is an honest valuation of a property, so the borrower does not overextend themselves with their higher loan amounts, and possibly get into trouble in the future if the balance of the mortgage outstanding is greater than the value of the house.

In addition, the FHA has seen that some appraisers are overvaluing properties and therefore placing the FHA in a serious predicament where they may have to pay out from their MMI Fund for loans that exceed the value of the property.

Who pays for this second appraisal. Well, the customer is supposed to bear the brunt of this expense, but in most cases the Lender is assuming this debt and covering the cost for the borrower. This is a good thing, but it is costing the Lenders a great deal of money from their bottom line. At some point, the Lenders may well pass on this cost to the borrower either in an upfront cost or by making it part of the total closing costs, so the borrowers would eventually pay for this cost. Borrowers beware!

What effect will this have on your Reverse Mortgage? Simply, the FHA will use the lower of the two appraisals to determine the actual loan amount they will lend you. In cases where the first appraisal comes in a bit high, and the customer is happy with the valuation and the loan amount, but the second appraisal comes in lower than the first, the second one, or lower of the two would be used to determine your loan amount, and this may make you very unhappy. In most cases this difference may be around

$10,000, which will reality may not have a tremendous impact on your loan amount, but in some cases that difference could make a big difference and impact your numbers to where you may not qualify anymore, or there may not be enough in the new loan amount to cover your current mortgage balance and/or expenses you needed to cover. In my office we had an instance where the difference was $170,000! Needless to say, the customer was not happy.

What alternatives does the borrower have? Not many! Really the only alternatives are to cancel the loan, or to accept the lower loan amount, and never look back. Sometimes the Lender can request a review of the appraisal, but please understand this is a very closed society, and they stick together like politicians. Therefore, in most cases the appraised value quoted will not be changed.

Most appraisers try to appraise a house at its actual value. But one has to understand that appraisals are a subjective value given by a licensed professional who determines a value using the best information available at the time, and it can change from day to day, and from individual to individual who is making this determination. Maybe someday, the internet will get to the point where appraisers will be eliminated altogether, and values will be obtained from data available on line. Let's not be very happy about this, because the same goes for Loan Officers. One day we all will be obsolete! I give it 3 years.

State of Nevada Living Will Lockbox

This is more of a Public Awareness Chapter in which I describe a little-known Program, which is free, set up by the State of Nevada for its citizens to Register their Health Care Directive in case of an emergency.

Just what is the Nevada Living Will Lockbox website?

The Nevada Lockbox is an electronic registry securely maintained by the Nevada Secretary of State website, which contains a copy of each document you submit for safekeeping to ensure your medical wishes are followed by your medical team, your Attorney, and anyone else you designate.

In the Lockbox, a citizen of Nevada can register their medical advance directives such as: The withholding of life sustaining treatment. A Durable Power of Attorney for Health Care decision. Or a Do Not resuscitate order.

Once you register, the Secretary of State will be responsible to you, your Health Care Provider, such as your Doctors, your Attorney, and any of your designated heirs in case of an emergency.

When you register, you will receive a wallet card which contains the registration number for access to the documents. Please make sure you carry this cad with you at all times in case of emergency. It is also very important for you to share a copy of this card, or the access information with your Doctors, with members of your family, and with your Attorney.

Now that we know how the Lockbox works, what is an Advance Directive?
An Advanced Directive is simply a Living Will document which you draft which gives instructions to your Doctors and Health Care Providers, and your family about your personal wishes on how you want them to take care of you in an emergency. In the Living Will you basically are making medical decisions for yourself before you are seriously ill or incapacitated. Also, a Living Will can provide specific instructions for end of life treatment. Thus, your decision to have

life sustaining treatment or not too have any care to keep you alive is your decision, and it will be respected. Remember, when in an emergency situation, Emergency Hospitals may not know what a patient's decision is, and then they try their best to keep you alive under all circumstances.

In case you change your mind at a later date, or wish to amend the Documents in the Lockbox, you are completely in control at all times, and can make any changes you wish. Just go to the Nevada Lockbox Website at: LivingWillLockbox.com and there are forms to make your changes. When you do make changes, don't forget to update your Doctors, Attorneys, and family members of your changes.

This is a free service, please look into it, and register your final wishes.

Living Will Lockbox
Nevada Secretary of State
555 E. Washington Ave. #5200
Las Vegas, NV 89101
775-684-5708
info@LivingWillLockbox.com
www.livingwilllockbox.com

Final Thoughts

To reiterate about my personal feelings about the Reverse Mortgage Program; I feel the Program is here to stay. The Government will continue to make changes in the coming years to better secure a positive position for themselves, so they do not lose money by doing the Reverse Mortgage loans to the Senior customers. The days of the reverse program being a "loan of last resort" is gone forever, it will stay a loan for the affluent and the wealthy Seniors.  More stringent guidelines will be implemented into the Program as the years pass, making it less desirable to the Seniors that need this money the most. And, the wealthy Seniors will benefit the most from the Program as they get better educated as to the benefits it offers them.

It is sad to believe that our Federal Congress passed a law several years ago giving up the power to control the Reverse Mortgage Program to the Director of HUD, the Housing and Urban Development of the Federal Housing Administration. Now, one person, and only one person has total authority to change any part of the Program as he/she sees fit even if it is not in the best interest of the Seniors.

On the Financial Assessment, my stance is that it only benefits the Reverse Mortgage Program and the MMI Fund. This change is what has made so many Seniors not qualify for a Reverse Mortgage since its inception. Not many numbers are made available by the Government as to the loans that have been denied or "adversed" as they call it, because those numbers are not good publicity for them. And most importantly, those numbers will be representative of the Seniors who most need this Program to have a decent retirement life, a decent life in their own homes.

Another way the Government will change the Program to better themselves in the future, at a cost to our Seniors, is by changing the "factor" which determines the amount of money you can get from the Reverse Mortgage Program. This has been changed several times in the last few years and each time they reduce the amount of the loan you can get. If you can remember just a few years ago, if you were 62 years old, you would be about 60% of the value of your home, now that "factor" has reduced the amount you receive to about 50% of the home's value, and today it's even less. If you keep on waiting to take out a

Reverse Mortgage, you may just get a little less in the years to come.

The Reverse Mortgage also serves one very important fact, and that is that when a Senior takes on a Reverse Mortgage on their house, they are using their own equity to live on, and are not so inclined to use other Government sources of funding to live on, thus saving the Government from taking care of them financially in a nursing home or an assisted living facility. Today several other Countries require their Senior population to take on a Reverse Mortgage product before the Government spends money on their care. Watch out, this may also be coming to the US in a future year.

As for me, I have a Reverse Mortgage on my own house (a Purchase Reverse Mortgage) and I am very happy every first of each month, when I do not have to make that monthly mortgage payment to the Bank, yet my friends all have to scrape their available funds to pay the Bank first, and live off what they have left. I use my money to have a meaningful life and do things which I would not otherwise be able to afford to do if I had to pay the Bank first.

I urge all of you who are over 62 years of age, to learn about this product, it may not be for you, but then again, it may be the one program which will allow you to live out your life in the manner in which you dreamed off. Educate yourself, and please get professional guidance about this program. Do not rely on what you have heard from 15 or 20 years ago, or what your landscaper told you, or what your great aunt knows about the product. Seek reliable, professional help before you make your final determination whether to get this Program or not. And, remember, it is a Federal Government Program which means it is not a scam or a way to hurt Seniors!

ABOUT THE AUTHOR
George Lagarde

After a 6 year stint as an Army MP, stationed mostly in West Point, I began my long Real Estate career in 1973, in Long Island, New York. In 1984, I opened a Mortgage Brokerage business. Shortly thereafter, in order to expand and bring greater value to my clients, I purchased a Century 21 Real Estate franchise. With both aspects of the Real Estate transaction covered I was able achieve my dream of owning my own business in something I loved to do; Real Estate and Mortgages.

My first introduction to HECM/Reverse Mortgages was with my mother; she owned a home in Florida with a small mortgage balance. She had been approached by a lender's representative urging her to take out a "reverse mortgage". Unfortunately, at that time I knew nothing about this particular mortgage product and thought he was trying to take advantage of her. He immediately recognized my product ignorance and he began sending me a tremendous amount of information about reverse mortgages. With this information, and some personal research, I found out just how good the program really was. So, my mother provided my first HECM/Reverse Mortgage experience. Later on, the agent who first approached my mother came to work with me.

After a few years, my mother's health deteriorated, and I decided to sell my businesses in New York and move to Florida to care for her. Until her passing four years later, my mother spoke often of how grateful she was for what her HECM Mortgage was able to afford her. Just before her death, she asked me what I was going to do with my life (I guess she was expecting me to say, I would return to New York), but I told her I was going to dedicate my efforts to helping Seniors, just like her, to have a more financially secure lives, and HUD's FHA HECM was my vehicle to help them. Today, I am fulfilling that promise to her.

My career has spanned the shift from the old Reverse Mortgage to the new FHA HECM; from my Mom's file so long ago to my efforts today with Seniors in Las Vegas, it is, and always has been, my goal:

Changing Lives...One Senior at a Time.

George Lagarde
702-845-4632
ReverseGeorge@gmail.com

ramcontent.com/pod-product-compliance
Source LLC
PA
10526
001B/461